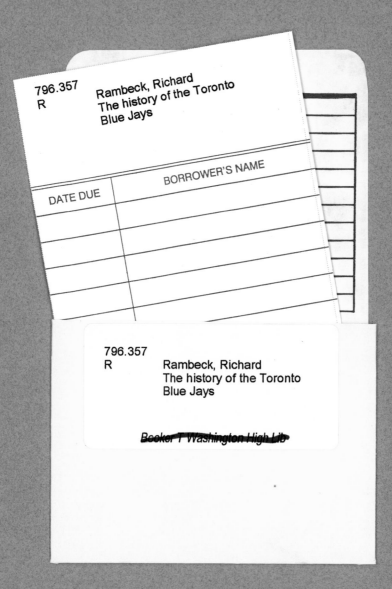

TORONTO

RICHARD RAMBECK

THE HISTORY OF THE

BLUE JAYS

CREATIVE EDUCATION

Published by Creative Education
123 South Broad Street, Mankato, Minnesota 56001
Creative Education is an imprint of The Creative Company

Designed by Rita Marshall
Editorial assistance by Tracey Cramer & John Nichols

Photos by: Allsport Photography, Focus on Sports, SportsChrome.

Library of Congress Cataloging-in-Publication Data

Rambeck, Richard.
The History of the Toronto Blue Jays / by Richard Rambeck.
p. cm. — (Baseball)
Summary: Highlights the key personalities and memorable games in the
history of the team that was formed in 1977 when the American League
expanded their circuit.
ISBN: 0-88682-928-3

1. Toronto Blue Jays (Baseball team)—History—Juvenile literature.
[1. Toronto Blue Jays (Baseball team)—History. 2. Baseball—History.]
I. Title. II. Series: Baseball (Mankato, Minn.)

GV875.T67R36   1999
796.357'64'09713541—dc21   97-9229

First edition

9 8 7 6 5 4 3 2 1

Centuries ago, travel was long and hard in the land known as America. Even by water, down the St. Lawrence River and across the five Great Lakes, the journey to the fertile Midwest could take months longer than planned. In the early 1700s, though, the French discovered that the Iroquois used a valuable shortcut, a 75-mile overland route northward that saved hundreds of miles in the journey from the first Great Lake, Ontario, to the third, Huron.

The French set up a mission, a fur trading post, and a fort at the beginning of the route. The settlement grew quickly, and it was named Toronto, from the Native American word

1 9 7 6

Peter Bavasi arranged the purchase of catcher Phil Roof's contract, making Roof the first official Blue Jay.

for "meeting place." This settlement has since exploded into a metropolis of approximately 3.8 million people. Toronto, located in the province of Ontario, is Canada's largest city. The one-time meeting place of early North American settlers is now a major center of trade, manufacturing, and finance.

Toronto is also home to a major league baseball team, the Blue Jays. The team hatched in 1976, when the American League expanded from 12 to 14 teams. Today the team is home to superstars such as Roger Clemens and Jose Cruz Jr., but when the Blue Jays first came into existence, the franchise had little talent with which to work. The team was owned by two huge Canadian companies, Imperial Trust Limited and Labatt's Breweries. The owners, who admitted they knew little about operating a sports franchise, knew they had to find a baseball expert to run the team. They turned to a 34-year-old who had spent his entire life around baseball: Peter Bavasi. He was the son of Buzzie Bavasi, who had helped build such clubs as the Brooklyn/Los Angeles Dodgers, the San Diego Padres, and the California Angels. The Toronto owners took a chance by hiring the younger Bavasi as executive vice president and general manager, but the gamble paid off.

BAVASI LAYS THE FOUNDATION

Peter Bavasi decided to build the Toronto team slowly, developing young talent in the farm system and, when possible, in the majors. "We decided to build a good farm system and to always try to get young players from other organizations," said Toronto scout Al LaMacchia. "Then we'd

Roger Clemens, an intense pitcher.

1 9 7 7

In Toronto's first game at Exhibition Stadium, Doug Ault hit two homers, sparking the team to victory.

go for the best athletes in our draft." Bavasi knew this was not the fastest way to build a winner. In fact, Seattle, the other expansion franchise, took a completely different route to assemble its team, building it around veterans who had been cast off by other teams. The Blue Jays, however, often would trade veteran players for young talent—talent that wasn't always quite ready for the big leagues, but soon would be. "You realize the importance of patience when you handle a team like ours," Bavasi said. "If you draft young, as we did, you have to bite the bullet. You don't make wholesale changes. If you do, you wind up mixing and matching—and eventually rebuilding."

The Blue Jays did bite the bullet their first three years, posting the worst record in baseball at the end of each season. Despite its numerous defeats, the Toronto team did produce some outstanding performances. During the first month of the team's existence, in April 1977, outfielder Otto Velez was named American League Player of the Month. Later that season, in September, the Blue Jays pounded Yankees pitching for a 19–3 victory in New York; this was the most runs scored by an opposing team in Yankee Stadium in more than 50 years. Infielder Ron Fairly was named to the American League All-Star team. In addition, shortstop Bob Bailor, first baseman Doug Ault, and pitcher Jerry Garvin were selected to the American League All-Rookie team. But perhaps Toronto's biggest highlight in its first year was fan attendance. More than 1.7 million people watched the Blue Jays play at their Exhibition Stadium home—a sign that the Toronto fans were in it for the long haul as well.

Because of the great fan support, the Blue Jays were a financial success from the beginning. The front office was able to use some of the money to beef up their scouting and player development efforts. Toronto scouts discovered their first gem during the early part of the 1978 season. Al LaMacchia and Bobby Mattick were in the stands at Eastern Illinois University to watch an outfielder who was playing for the visiting team, Southern Illinois. LaMacchia and Mattick wanted to see Dave Stieb hit and play the outfield. They did, and they were disappointed. Stieb just wasn't a great hitter. LaMacchia and Mattick were about to leave when fate entered the picture.

1 9 7 8

Roy Howell was selected as the Blue Jays' lone representative in the All-Star Game.

The Southern Illinois team was a little short on pitchers that day, so the manager called Stieb in from the outfield to take the mound. Out of curiosity more than anything else, the two Blue Jays' scouts stayed around to watch Stieb pitch. Had they known Stieb's background, though, they might have left. Stieb had never pitched at any level before playing in college, not even in Little League. He had never really wanted to pitch, because he was worried it might damage his arm. He occasionally pitched for Southern Illinois— mainly because the team needed him—which was the case the day LaMacchia and Mattick were in the stands.

On that day Stieb, the marginal outfield prospect, became Stieb, the red-hot pitching prospect. The Toronto scouts couldn't believe what they saw. "Stieb knocked our eyeballs out," said Mattick, who was director of player development at the time. "He was absolutely overpowering. We hadn't

Blue Jays ace Dave Stieb.

Slick-fielding shortstop Alfredo Griffin.

liked him as a hitter, but he sure opened our eyes when he started pitching." The Blue Jays were impressed enough to select Stieb in the amateur draft that June.

Stieb was anxious to sign a professional contract, but he couldn't understand why the Blue Jays were so interested in him as a pitcher, a position he had hardly played. "It was hard for me to fathom why they wanted me to be something I wasn't," Stieb said. "I don't think I even knew how to figure an ERA [earned-run average] in those days. I still felt I could make it as a hitter." Stieb the pitcher spent the rest of the 1978 season in Toronto's minor-league system. As far as the Blue Jays were concerned, he was a natural as a pitcher and would soon be in the major leagues. "We didn't monkey around with his mechanics at all," Mattick said. "He has the same delivery today as he had then. He was one in a million. He had such a desire to excel."

It was that desire that carried Stieb to the majors near the end of the 1979 season, in only his second year as a pro. Soon he was one of the top pitchers on the Toronto staff, someone on whom the struggling team came to rely. "Dave is the most intense person I've ever met," said his agent, Bob LaMonte. "He's so tight, and it's that tightness that makes him such a great pitcher. He was asked to be a leader at 21. You'd have to be Gandhi to handle some of the pressure Dave's had, and Gandhi couldn't have pitched for the Toronto Blue Jays."

Stieb was a quality pitcher from the time he made the majors. However, the Blue Jays weren't a quality team. Toronto finished with a 53–109 record in 1979, despite the efforts of Stieb and shortstop Alfredo Griffin, who was voted Co-

1 9 7 9

First baseman John Mayberry led Toronto in home runs (21) and RBIs (74).

Rookie of the Year in the American League. Griffin set club records for hits (179), runs scored (81), triples (10), and stolen bases (21). In addition, his .279 batting average was the best among all American League shortstops.

Griffin and Stieb may have been tops, but Toronto was a last-place club that had registered the second-worst start of any expansion team in history during its first three years. "About the middle of the '79 season," admitted a disappointed Peter Bavasi, "the club spirit began to deteriorate. The players were discouraged. Their confidence was shattered." Bavasi decided to fire manager Roy Hartsfield and hire Bobby Mattick as the new skipper. At first, the 64-year-old Mattick didn't want the job, and he told Bavasi so—twice. But Bavasi kept asking, and Mattick finally accepted.

Mattick restored the players' confidence, and the Blue Jays improved, winning 67 games in 1980 and actually contending for first place during the second half of the strike-shortened 1981 season. After two years as manager, Mattick was promoted to executive coordinator of baseball operations for the Blue Jays. His replacement as manager was Bobby Cox, who would continue to build on what Mattick had started in Toronto.

The Blue Jays weren't pennant contenders in Cox's first year, 1982, but they did capture the fancy of their partisan supporters by winning 44 of 81 home games. Young second baseman Damaso Garcia led the club with a .310 batting average and set new team records for hits (185), runs scored (89), and stolen bases (54). First baseman Willie Upshaw had an excellent year with 21 home runs, 75 runs batted in, and a team-record 14 game-winning hits. But the best Blue

Under new manager Bobby Mattick, the Blue Jays finished with their best record to date, 67–95.

Center fielder Lloyd Moseby led Toronto in RBIs (92) and bases-on-balls (78).

Jay of them all in 1982 was Dave Stieb. He led the American League in shutouts (five), complete games (19), and innings pitched (288.33). "I don't think he has any weaknesses," claimed Baltimore Orioles manager Joe Altobelli.

Stieb had the respect of the entire American League, and that would soon be the case with the young Blue Jays, who just kept improving under Bobby Cox. The 1983 team finished with the first winning record in franchise history (89–73), which was good enough to put the Jays in fourth place in the powerful American League East. Stieb and Jim Clancy anchored the pitching staff, but a trio of young outfielders drew much of the attention.

JAYS OUTFIELD IS OUT OF THIS WORLD

There have been few more closely matched trios of outfielders in baseball history than Toronto's Jesse Barfield, George Bell, and Lloyd Moseby. Bobby Cox called them "one of the best young outfields in the game. All three of them can throw, run, and hit with power." And they were all virtually the same age. Bell was born October 21, 1959. Eight days later, Barfield came into the world. And seven days after that, Moseby made his appearance.

The youngest of the three, Moseby was the first to play like a superstar. In 1983, he batted .315, became the first Blue Jay ever to score 100 runs in a season (104), and stole 27 bases. But it was the center fielder's speed and ability with the glove that impressed teammates and opponents. "With that guy [Moseby] in center field," said Cleveland manager Pat Corrales, "anything in the outfield can be caught."

First baseman Willie Upshaw.

The durable Jesse Barfield.

But Moseby wasn't always a great outfielder. "He used to be brutal in the Instructional League," said Barfield of Moseby. "We still tease him about it. We had to be out on the field about 9:30 or 10 [a.m.], but he'd be out there at 8:30 [a.m.] . . . taking grounders, flies, sliding to catch the ball. To see him in 1978 and see him now—he's a Gold Glove now, no question about it."

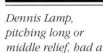

Dennis Lamp, pitching long or middle relief, had a remarkable 11–0 season for Toronto.

And no question about it, the Blue Jays were a good team in 1984. The problem was that the Detroit Tigers had been outstanding all season long. Detroit won 35 of their first 40 games in 1984, racing out to a big lead over the second-place Jays, who still had a remarkable 28–14 record. Toronto, despite 26 homers and 87 RBIs from George Bell, couldn't catch Detroit—who went on to claim the AL East, then the American League pennant, and finally the World Series. The Blue Jays wound up second in the division with a mark of 89–73, their highest finish ever, and they vowed to overtake the Tigers in 1985.

Once the next season started, it was obvious the Blue Jays were the top team in the American League East. In addition to their fabulous outfield, the Jays had a new young star in shortstop Tony Fernandez, who was so good the team could trade longtime standout Alfredo Griffin. Pitchers Dave Stieb, Jim Clancy, and ace reliever Tom Henke all had solid years. As a result, Toronto assumed sole possession of first place in the division on May 20, 1985, and never gave it up. Late in the season, when the team seemed on the verge of falling into second place, veteran pitcher Doyle Alexander stepped in and kept the team on top. Toronto outlasted the second-place New York Yankees

Slugger George Bell (pages 18-19).

and won the division with a 99–62 record, the second-best mark in all of baseball.

The Blue Jays, who had gone from worst to first in the AL East in just three years, were favored to best the West Division champion Kansas City Royals in the American League Championship Series. In the first game of the series, Stieb pitched masterfully in a 6–1 Toronto victory. "The way Stieb pitched tonight," said Kansas City center fielder Willie Wilson, "you wonder how he ever loses." The Royals may have been wondering if they had any chance to win the series after the Blue Jays took three of the first four games. With Toronto only one victory from becoming the first Canadian team ever to advance to the World Series, the Royals destroyed the Jays' hopes by winning three straight games to claim the American League pennant. "We gave it our best shot, I'll say that," a disappointed Bobby Cox said.

Cox would not return as manager for the 1986 season. In four years he had taken the Blue Jays from nowhere to the top of the American League East. Now, he said after the 1985 season, it was time for him to move on. The man who was voted Manager of the Year by *The Sporting News* accepted the job as general manager of the National League's Atlanta Braves. In Cox's place, the Blue Jays hired Jimy Williams, whose job it would be to take the team to the World Series.

1 9 8 6

Jesse Barfield (above) and Tony Fernandez became the first Blue Jays players to win Gold Glove awards.

BELL RINGS IN MVP NUMBERS

Williams inherited a lot of talent when he took over the Blue Jays, but the team slumped from first in the AL East in 1985 to fourth in 1986, mainly because the pitching staff struggled with injuries and ineffectiveness. Dave Stieb lost his first six games and wound up 7–12. But while the pitching was substandard, the hitting was tremendous. Jesse Barfield led the American League in homers with 40, and George Bell cracked 31 more, including an amazing 15 game-winners. Bell rang up even better numbers in 1987. The slugger from the Dominican Republic slammed 47 homers, drove in an American League-leading 134 runs, batted .308, and registered team highs in hits (188) and runs scored (111). For his efforts, Bell was voted the American League Most Valuable Player.

California Angels manager Gene Mauch called Bell "the most intimidating hitter in the league." Los Angeles Dodgers scout Mel Didier claimed that Bell "comes off the bench swinging. You throw the ball two feet outside, and he might just step out and hammer the pitch." Bell had gained the respect of the players, managers, and fans, but the Blue Jays' slugger was not a particularly popular player, except in the Toronto clubhouse. Bell, who grew up speaking Spanish, was hesitant to use his halting English during his early years in the major leagues. Because Bell didn't talk much, many people thought he was an angry man with a chip on his shoulder, but his teammates knew otherwise.

"People are always asking me about George, even umpires," said Alfredo Griffin, Bell's good friend. "Just the other day, Reggie Jackson was asking me what kind of guy he [Bell] is. Well, I know he looks like a mean person, but he's not. He's a nice person, a wonderful guy. He knows what it is to work hard."

Bell, who admits that he can be a hard person to know,

1 9 8 7

Jimmy Key led the Blue Jays with 17 victories and was runner-up for the Cy Young Award.

Hard-throwing closer Tom Henke.

seemed more at peace with himself after his great 1987 season. "Everybody matures sometime," Bell explained. "I'm much more relaxed. I've got a wife and three kids, a good family. I'm making good money, and we've got a team that's going to win."

The Blue Jays did win, but they didn't win division championships. Toronto seemed headed for the 1987 AL East title, but Detroit caught and passed the Blue Jays during the final week of the season. Toronto posted another winning record in 1988, but the Boston Red Sox walked away with the division championship. The Blue Jays were discouraged, but they vowed to rise to the top the next season. Yet Toronto started very slowly in 1989, winning only 12 of its first 36 games.

Pitcher Dave Stieb led the Toronto club with four shutouts, 16 wins, and a 3.04 ERA.

Jimy Williams, having failed in his mission to reach the World Series, was fired as manager and replaced by Cito Gaston. With the low-key Gaston at the helm, the Blue Jays started to win. Bell, Barfield, and third baseman Kelly Gruber carried a great deal of the load, but Toronto also received production from a new weapon. Sweet-swinging first baseman Fred McGriff provided the power for the Blue Jays' rise to the top of the standings.

McGRIFF MEASURES UP

McGriff wound up leading the American League in homers in 1989 with 36, but that feat didn't come as a real surprise to his Toronto teammates, who had been watching the powerful slugger hammer tape-measure shots for years. During spring training in 1985, McGriff slammed a shot that would have traveled more than 500 feet had it not hit a tower beyond the fence. "I played with [Mickey] Mantle in his last years," said Bobby Cox. "I saw him hit a few long ones, and I saw Frank Howard hit a few. But I've got to say, I never saw a ball like the one this kid hit. It was still going up when it hit the tower."

George Bell hit three home runs on Opening Day (April 3)—the first major league player to do so.

During the 1987 regular season, McGriff's first in the majors, he hit a home run 480 feet in New York's Yankee Stadium. "I've never seen anything like that, and I doubt whether I'll ever see anything like that again," said Toronto's Willie Upshaw.

McGriff, who hit 20 homers in 1987 and 34 in 1988, seemed amazed he had so much power. "I'm just as surprised as anybody when the ball jumps off my bat, but I can't get too aggressive," McGriff said during the 1989 season. "I'd be happy to get 25 homers every year. You know how tough that is to do? I look at Darryl Strawberry [of the New York Mets], whom I admire. He's got a perfect swing— perfect. But he hits 39 homers, and people don't think that's enough. Look, it's not like I don't know what I'm doing, like I'm not proud of what I'm doing. But I just let it come. I don't anticipate."

McGriff may not have anticipated homers, but his teammates anticipated success for the young slugger. "He has a good eye and power, a combination you don't see too often anymore," said Lloyd Moseby. Toronto pitcher Jimmy Key claimed McGriff could hit 50 home runs in a season. "He might," Key said. "Pitching's different—it's better, deeper. But Fred's a hitter, too."

Thanks to McGriff's power and Dave Stieb's outstanding pitching, the Blue Jays surpassed the Baltimore Orioles near the end of the 1989 season to claim the AL East Division crown. Toronto then lost the pennant to the Oakland Athletics, the eventual World Series champs, four games to one in the American League Championship Series.

FLYING HIGH IN THE '90S

Third baseman Kelly Gruber hit for the cycle (a single, double, triple, and home run) against Kansas City, April 16.

The year 1991 saw a repeat of '89: The Blue Jays again won their division title, but were unable to defeat the Minnesota Twins, the eventual World Series champs who beat the Jays in the American League Championship Series, three games to one on Toronto's own turf.

Despite the defeat, the Blue Jays felt confident they were on the verge of becoming the first Canadian team to play in a World Series. And they were right.

In 1992, the Jays again clinched the AL East Division title—this time they beat the Oakland Athletics in the championship series—and earned Canada's first-ever appearance in the World Series against the Atlanta Braves.

It was a nail-biter. By game five, Toronto held the lead three games to two, despite close calls in games two, three, and four. Game six went into extra innings. Finally, in the 11th inning, Dave Winfield hit a double that brought in two runs. However, the Braves immediately answered with another run—plus they had a runner on third with two outs. With the pressure on, Atlanta's speedy Otis Nixon dropped a bunt down the first base line. Mike Timlin, the Jays' pitcher, jumped off the mound, grabbed the ball, and with lightning speed, fired it to Joe Carter at first base for the final out. Canada finally had its first World Series championship.

Jose Cruz Jr., a rising star (pages 26-27).

*Joe Carter belted
two home runs
in one inning
against the
Baltimore Orioles
on October 3.*

"What an honor it is to be a part of this team," said Winfield. "This means an awful lot to the people of Canada. I'm just so happy we could make it happen for them."

The Blue Jays' momentum carried over into the 1993 season. Although several key players from the 1992 World Series were gone, the team had one new face who would play a pivotal role: designated hitter Paul Molitor. He had spent 15 years with the Milwaukee Brewers and gave the Jays yet another productive bat in the lineup. "Paul is what I call a professional hitter," explained Cito Gaston. "He's very smart, and at 37 years old he still has one of the quickest bats in the league."

Once again, Toronto stormed to the division championship. The Blue Jays then defeated the Chicago White Sox in the American League Championship Series, four games to two. After claiming the pennant, they were off to face the Philadelphia Phillies in their second World Series appearance in two years.

Again it was a close series. The turning point came when the Blue Jays scored the final three runs in the eighth inning of game four. The 15–14 win set a record for number of runs scored in a single World Series game. In game six, the Blue Jays came from behind in what some people say was the most dramatic finish in World Series play: Joe Carter smacked a three-run homer in the bottom of the ninth inning to win the game 8–6 and clinch the series, four games to two. But it was Molitor who was voted MVP. He had 12 hits in 24 at-bats, a record-tying 10 runs, and 24 total bases (one short of another record).

Some people wondered if the Blue Jays could have done

28

it again in 1994. No one will ever know; the season was canceled midway by a players' strike. When play resumed in 1995, it was obvious the Blue Jays had lost their championship momentum. The team finished last in the American League Central, 30 games behind the first place Boston Red Sox.

Blue Jays management got serious about rebuilding the team after the 1995 season ended, but clearly it would take time. The Toronto offense had been decimated by several free agent losses. Stars such as Molitor, Roberto Alomar, and Devon White had all left, weakening the Jays lineup considerably. The years 1996 and 1997 proved to be disappointing for Toronto, as the team struggled to post 74 and 76 wins. Gaston was fired at the end of the '97 season, and now a new era in Blue Jay baseball appears ready to begin.

1 9 9 6

Paul Molitor smashed five hits in one game versus the Kansas City Royals (September 4).

BLUE JAYS TARGET RETURN TO GLORY

Toronto fans' hopes for a return to championship form rest largely in the hands of two men: pitcher "Rocket" Roger Clemens and outfielder Jose Cruz Jr.

Formerly with the Boston Red Sox, Clemens signed with Toronto before the 1997 season. The three-time Cy Young Award winner was rumored to be past his prime at age 35, but Clemens and the Blue Jays thought differently. "Not many power pitchers still have the good fastball by the time they reach their mid 30s," observed Blue Jay teammate Pat Hentgen. "But Roger is not your average guy. He's made of different stuff than you or I." The supposedly aging Clemens took the American League by storm in 1997, winning 21

Slugging young outfielder Shawn Green.

The Toronto SkyDome. 31

games, notching 292 strikeouts, and posting an ERA of 2.05; all league bests. "The Rocket Man is back," muttered Chicago White Sox slugger Frank Thomas after facing Clemens. "He's just unhittable right now." Clemens captured his fourth Cy Young Award for his brilliant '97 campaign.

The other integral piece of the Blue Jay resurgence will be Jose Cruz Jr., a man barely 20 years old but with a world of talent. The son of former Houston Astros great Jose Cruz Sr., Cruz Jr. began his career with the Seattle Mariners, but was dealt to the Blue Jays midway through the '97 season. The multitalented Cruz immediately gave Toronto fans a glimpse of the future, finishing his rookie season with 26 homers and 68 RBIs. "That Cruz kid is a real jewel," observed New York Yankees manager Joe Torre. "He hits a ton, he can run, he can throw, and he's got great instincts in the field."

The Blue Jays also have strong talent to surround their two stars. The 1996 Cy Young Award winner Pat Hentgen and hard-throwing Juan Guzman provide pitching strength, while Joe Carter, first baseman Carlos Delgado, and third baseman Ed Sprague form a fearsome offensive threat. This talented Blue Jays squad has one goal: to give its fans a chance to cheer another world championship team in Toronto's beautiful SkyDome, an incredible ballpark with a roof that can open or close to form either an open-air stadium or a dome. With Clemens and Cruz Jr. leading the way, the sky's the limit for the resurgent Blue Jays.

1 9 9 8

With Carlos Delgado's 30 home runs the previous season, he was expected to spark the Blue Jays' attack.